Crash Course
In Bible memorization

by
Dan Vis

Copyright © 2023 by Dan Vis
All rights reserved
including the right of reproduction
in whole or in part in any form.

All Scripture quotations are from the
King James Version of the Bible
Emphasis supplied unless otherwise indicated.

ISBN: 978-1-958155-05-9

Published by FAST Missions
111 2nd Street
Kathryn, ND 58049

Additional copies of this book are available by visiting us at WWW.FAST.ST

Dedication

This book is dedicated to Eric, one of my earliest Christian brothers, who started his whole journey to Christ by memorizing one verse.

Table of Contents

Chapter 1:   The Foundational Reason 1

Chapter 2:   Tips to Success 6

Chapter 3:   The Secret to Retention 11

Chapter 4:   Remembering References 16

Chapter 5:   Engine Magic 22

Chapter 6:   Continuing On 28

Chapter 7:   Spreading Sparks 34

Bonus: The Minute Memorizer 38

Crash Course
Preface

Ever wanted to know how to memorize the Word of God effectively? To have dozens, even hundreds of verses fresh, and right on the tip of your tongue? To have the quiver of your heart filled with arrows from God's Word—ready for the Master's use? It can happen you know! Thousands today are using the simple keys just ahead to memorize Scripture, and now you can too!

This small book covers several important things: first, why you should memorize, and then second, how to do it effectively. By the time you have finished this brief Crash Course in Bible memorization, you will know how to use a verse pack, maintain longterm retention of verses, remember references, and more. You will also learn a few tips on the single most important key to success: consistency. And as a bonus, we will throw in a few suggestions as to what verses you should memorize first!

So dive in with an eager heart, and God will be sure to bless.

The Foundational Reason
Chapter 1

People have a lot of great reasons for memorizing Scripture. Some want to be able to answer people's questions with God's Word rather than their own. Some want to use Scripture in resisting temptation, like Jesus did. Others want to be able to claim specific promises when praying. Others know it will make them more effective when preaching or teaching. And some want to keep Scripture inside so they can meditate on it at any time through the day. These are all good biblical reasons to memorize.

But it raises an important question: Why do YOU want to memorize Scripture? Visualize yourself down the road a few months. Maybe a year or two. You have been following the instructions we are going to be teaching you consistently, and you now have dozens, or even hundreds of verses memorized. Word-perfect. Complete with reference. Ready at a moment's notice, at the slightest whisper of the Holy Spirit.

How might having that kind of internalized Scripture change your life? How might it impact your day to day walk with God? Understanding what motivates you is important. And keeping that reason you want to memorize fixed in your mind as you go forward, is going to help you.

But I'd like to suggest there's an even more foundational reason to memorize, than any of the ones I've suggested already.

And it's simply this: God commanded it!

Study the Bible carefully, and you will find dozens of explicit commands to memorize Scripture. It uses phrases like "lay it up", "write it in your heart", "hold it fast", "keep in memory", "let thine heart retain", "forget it not", and many more. I could give you a long list of verses, but for the sake of brevity I will assume you have seen at least some of them. But I can say this, by my estimate, there are more verses commanding us to memorize, than verses calling us to read, listen to, or even study the Bible—combined! And by a ration of at least two to one! That's a lot of verses...

Here's why that is important.

First, to stick with Scripture memory over the long haul, it is going to take some commitment. You have got to be determined. You need to set your mind, like a flint—that you will continue memorizing no matter what. In time, Scripture memory will become the "joy and rejoicing" of your heart (Jeremiah 15:16). But until then—it will be commitment that holds you. The question cannot be what attracts me, interests me, appeals to me at the moment. The question has to be: Does God want me memorizing His Word? Is Scripture memory a part of His plan for my life? And if so, it becomes a simple question of obedience.

But it also means this: if it is commanded, then you can be sure God will help you do it! You've probably heard the saying: all His biddings, are enablings. Or this one: every command is a promise. Both are true! God never asks us to do anything without also supplying the power we need to obey. You can count on it. That means if you set out to memorize Scripture because God has commanded it, you can be 100% confident He will give you the grace you need to succeed.

Knowing God is certain to help us, is so important, I would like to suggest a first memory verse:

Philippians 4:13
I can do all things through Christ which strengtheneth me.

Try repeating that out loud a few times until you can say it without looking. It should just take a minute or two to learn. Tomorrow, we'll talk more about how to actually memorize, but you should be able to get this first verse learned with no trouble at all. Which just goes to show how easy memorizing really is.

And if that old devil comes along whispering in your ear that memorization is too hard, your memory is not any good, or any other nonsense of that sort, just throw this verse right back at him! That's part of what we're memorizing for, isn't it? To use it when we need it?

All right, this marks the end of our first study. You now know the biggest reason to memorize, and hopefully, you've got your first verse learned. Tomorrow we'll pick right up where we left off, with more tips on how to memorize successfully...

The Foundational Reason
Study Questions

What are some of the most common reasons people have for wanting to memorize Scripture?

What is your reason for wanting to memorize? How could it potentially change your life?

What is an even more foundational reason for memorizing Scripture?

What are some of the phrases the Bible uses to talk about memorization?

What does it take to stick with Scripture memory over the long haul? How can knowing memorization is commanded help with this?

If Scripture memory is commanded, what can we know God will do for sure?

What should you do if the devil comes along whispering in your ear that memorization is too hard?

Additional Notes:

Tips to Success
Chapter 2

Memorizing is not really that hard. It's basically just repeating the first phrase of a verse several times until you can say it easily. Then you add another phrase and repeat—until you can do both. And then another phrase, and then another still, until you've got the whole thing learned. You can learn short verses in a matter of minutes. Long passages just take a bit longer.

The problem, actually, is not our memorizer—it's our forgetter. You see, the brain has a remarkably good ability to discard information it doesn't think it needs. And I'm quite glad for that—after all, most of us have experienced plenty of stuff we'd just as soon forget, haven't we? In other words, the problem is not really learning a verses, it's when those verses we've memorized start to slip. If you memorized Philippians 4:13 yesterday, it has likely vanished away, unless you kept working at it through the day. Which leads right to my tip for today: keep your verses with you.

When I first started, I did all my memorizing using a small verse pack I kept in my pocket. And it worked great! Mine was leather, had two inside pockets and a clear outside pocket. I would put recently memorized verses in one inside pocket, blank cards in the other, and kept my current verse in that outside pocket. On each card, I'd put the words of the verse on one side, and the reference on the back.

Because I had my verse pack with me, I could pull it out any time I had a few minutes and work on a verse: walking down a sidewalk, sitting at a stoplight, waiting in line, etc. I could set it on the dash of my car when driving, on my desk when working, on my kitchen window sill when doing dishes. By using such moments carefully, I was able to learn hundreds of verses without having to set aside any special times for memorizing. You can get a verse pack just like this, and cards, in our Online Store or at many Christian bookstores.

Nowadays, most people have a smart phone in their pocket—and you can use that to do something similar if you like. In the TOOLS section of our website (*WWW.FAST.ST*), you'll find a free digital "Verse Pack" designed to help you store verses you are working on, so you can review them whenever you have spare moment. Just pull out your phone, and work on your current verse. I definitely recommend giving it a quick look.

Regardless of which approach you use, it is this process of frequently memorizing, forgetting, and then re-memorizing again, that finally gets a verse to stick. Each time you relearn it, the verse comes back a little quicker, and stays a little longer. Eventually, your brain figures out it's something you're supposed to remember, and you simply stop forgetting it.

So that's my suggestion for today. Either write out Philippians 4:13 on a card and keep it with you. Or put our digital verse pack on your phone and get that first verse entered there. If you learned it yesterday, but have forgotten it since, take a moment to relearn it right now. See if it isn't even easier to learn the second time around. Here it is for your convenience:

> *Philippians 4:13*
> *I can do all things through Christ which strengtheneth me.*

Then, all through the day, take out that card (or your phone) every chance you can and learn that verse again. And again, and again, and again. Keep working at it, until it finally starts to stick. That's when you really have that verse memorized.

In our next section, we'll talk about how to retain your verses longterm. Permanently in fact...

Tips to Success
Study Questions

For most people, the difficulty is not actually our memorizer. What is it? Explain.

What is a "verse pack" and how can it help you memorize?

Explain in basic terms how you use a verse pack:

What modern day tool can you use as an alternative to a physical verse pack?

Where can you go to check out our digital verse pack?

Explain the process by which you get your brain to stop forgetting your verses:

Additional Notes:

The Secret to Retention
Chapter 3

As I mentioned yesterday, for most people, the hard part about memorizing Scripture is not actually the memorizing, but the retaining. An average person can memorize a verse in 10 or 20 minutes quite easily, but he will then go on to forget it just a few hours later. If he wants the verse to stick, he will need to work at it, learning it over and over again.

But the real goal is longterm retention.

Solomon once said: "Let thine heart retain my words: keep my commandments, and live. Get wisdom, get understanding: forget it not" (Proverbs 4:4-5). The question is how do we do that?

The answer is simple: daily review. To ensure longterm retention you just need to review your verse once each day for two months. Let me say that again: every day for two months.

How often? Every day.
How long? Two months.

That's the crux of it—every day for two months. (See how repetition works?)

In terms of memorizing, once you get a verse to the point it is sticking pretty good, write the date on it and move it to the inside pocket of your verse pack and put a new verse in the outside pocket. If you are using our phone app, you can do the equivalent by moving the verse from your verse pack to our daily review tool called the Review Engine (also in the TOOLS section of our site). Either way, the idea is to move on to your next verse and start learning it, while simultaneously remembering to review recently learned verses regularly for awhile.

At least once every day. For two months. :)

Here's how you do it. Let's assume you are using physical cards. Once each morning, simply take 5 or 10 minutes and flip through the cards in your recently memorized verses group, and go through them one by one. Look at the reference side, and then try to say the words of the verses from memory, without looking. Then, flip the card over to check your accuracy. Try not to miss a day!

Once the date indicates a verse has been in your daily review for two months, move it to a permanent back review file that you keep at home. Work through these verses as often as you can—we recommend once a week, at first. Later, after you have accumulated several hundred verses, you can start moving some of your oldest verses to a section for monthly review.

In general, back review verses need to be reviewed at least once a month no matter how long you've known them—if you want to keep them fresh and sharp on the tip of your tongue. But if you do notice a verse starting to get a bit rusty, just give it some extra attention. Put it back in with your other daily review verses for a week or so. It'll polish up quite nicely.

If you want to try our digital Review Engine, it's even easier. We'll keep track of everything for you. Just login once a day and review your verses. We randomize the verses you see each day and advance each verse from daily, to weekly, to monthly, automatically—at just the right pace to maintain your verses indefinitely. And if you miss a verse it's easy to note that and we'll start showing it more often automatically. I'll talk more about this tool a bit later in the course. But it's surprisingly powerful—and at some point you're definitely going to want to give it a try.

In closing today, allow me to suggest a second verse for you. Genesis 1:1. There's actually two reasons for choosing this verse—beside the fact it is short, easy, and familiar to most people. One, is to remind you of the creative power of God's Word. He spoke, and our entire world burst into existence, instantly. That's how powerful Scripture really is. And that power is still present in every verses you internalize.

Chew on that while you learn this verse...

Here's the verse, if you don't have a Bible handy. Note that if you are viewing this verse online, you can click a verse any place you see it highlighted to go straight to our online Bible, and there you will find an easy option to move that verse straight into our digital Verse Pack. Or advance it to the Review Engine. But for now, let's just see if you can get this verse learned:

Genesis 1:1
In the beginning God created the heaven and the earth.

I'll give you the other reason for memorizing this verse near the end of the course. So do your best to learn it! You will be glad you did.

And next up, I've got some keys to remembering references. You are going to love them...

The Secret to Retention
Study Questions

What is the real goal of memorization?

What is the secret to never forgetting a verse?

How often should you review a verse? And for how long?

What should you do with a verse after it has been in your daily review for two months?

How often do you need to go over your back review verses?

What should you do if a verse starts to get a little rusty?

How much power is there, really, in the Word of God?

Additional Notes:

Remembering References
Chapter 4

Have you ever lost your keys? Maybe you were racing out the door, only to realize you don't know where your car keys are. Or you were out and about and accidentally locked the keys inside your car. Neither one of these is a pleasant experience. We need keys to access whatever those keys are designed to unlock.

References are like the keys to the verses you learn. Remembering where your verses are found is important!

It's also one of the most common problems new memorizers struggle with.

Fortunately, I know a couple things that will really help. Some people recommend coming up with elaborate triggers to try and link the numbers to the verse--but in my experience, remembering the trigger for each verse is just as hard as remembering the reference! And it's not really necessary.

The suggestions ahead are simple and they work. Give them an honest try, and you never have to lose your keys again. Well, your references...

Reference Glue

I don't know exactly what to call this first tip, but "reference glue" is as good a name as any. It's a simple technique I use whenever I'm having trouble getting a verse and a reference linked together. I started doing it years ago without really thinking about it, and it never occurred to me to mention it to others for a long time. But it definitely helps, and especially so, when you are first learning a new verse.

Let's say you are having trouble remembering exactly how Philippians 4:13 begins. Jut take the reference and the first few words and repeat them quickly 10 or 20 times, like this:

Philippians 4:13   I can do
Philippians 4:13   I can do
Philippians 4:13   I can do
Philippians 4:13   I can do
Philippians 4:13   I can do

I don't say the whole verse, just the first couple words. But I say it with the reference multiple times at a rapid pace. It's enough to get me into the swing of the verse and I can easily finish it from there, without much trouble. Basically, it glues the reference to the verse.

You can do it with old verses too. Any time your verse starts separating from the reference, give it a little glue. And keep applying glue liberally as often as needed. It won't take long until your reference and verse gets stuck back together again.

The Sandwich Principle

If you have done some of our other classes at FAST you may have heard this one before. We've been teaching it for years. Basically, the sandwich principle simply reminds us to make it a habit to always review our verses the same way: reference, verse, reference. Like two slices of bread with the good stuff in between.

I'm not talking about doing this every time you read or share a verse with someone. I'm simply talking specifically about making it a rule to always do your review the exact same way, every time: reference, then the verse, then the reference again. And preferably out loud. Like this:

> *Philippians 4:13*
> *I can do all things through Christ which strengtheneth me.*
> *Philippians 4:13*

Doing it this way cements the reference to the verse and the verse to the reference. So if you hear someone say Philippians 4:13, you immediately think "I can do all things...". And if you hear the words of the verse, your mind immediately jumps to the reference at the end. Essentially, the goal is to memorize the reference and the verse together!

So again, make it a habit to always sandwich your verses (and out loud) when doing your personal review.

Reverse Drills

Here's my last suggestion. It's what I call reverse drills, and you'll find this one especially good for keeping references sharp on all those old verses in your back review.

Normally, when you write out your verses on cards, you put the reference on one side of the card and the words of the verse (without the reference) on the other. Then, when doing your review, you look at the reference side, say the verse, then flip the card over and check your self to make sure you quoted it word-perfect. Basically, you use your cards like flash cards.

To do reverse drills, you simply reverse the cards. That is, you look at the verse side, and try to say the reference. Then flip it over and check yourself. It actually goes really quick and is a lot of fun--you'll probably enjoy it. So if you find yourself struggling with references, try doing your daily review both ways every day, for a week or two. You'll be amazed how quickly it can sharpen up your reference recall!

Note that our online Review Engine has a built in system for doing reverse drills that makes all this a snap. And you can switch between random order and book order review without having to shuffle or sort a single card! Which is one huge plus to using a digital tool like this! Don't misunderstand me. Physical cards works great. I used 3x5 cards for years and learned hundreds of verses with no problem. But I genuinely love the flexibility of our Review Engine!

In summary, if you want to remember references, use lot's of reference glue when first learning a verse, use the sandwich method whenever you work through your daily review, and throw in lots of extra reverse drills to keep those back verses nice and sharp. And if you are doing it all online, be sure to shuffle things up.

That's about it!

Now before I get into our last two keys to memorization, I want to take a moment to talk more about the advantages of a good digital tool. Coming up next...

Remembering References
Study Questions

What common memorization problem is like losing your keys?

What is the problem with using elaborate triggers to remember a reference?

Explain what each of the following techniques are and how to use them to remember your references:

- Reference Glue

- The Sandwich Principle

- Reference Drills

What is one advantage of using our Review Engine over only using cards?

Which technique above is especially important for the following stages in the memorization process?

- Initial Memorization

- Daily Review Verses

- Back Review Verses

Additional Notes:

Engine Magic
Chapter 5

I've mentioned our online tools a couple times already, but before introducing our last two memorization keys, I want to say just a bit more about how digital tools can strengthen your memorization.

Now if you are not big on computers, that's fine. Feel free to stick with paper cards, to manage your review. I memorized my first 1000 verses that way, and it worked great. In other words, today's reading is something of a "bonus" suggestion. It's helpful, but not required to succeed in memorization. Everything else I've shared, however, is indispensable.

But memory tools can make a difference. That's point number two. In surveying our community about their memorization practices we made a not-so-surprising discovery about the connection between digital tools and successful memorization:

Verses Memorized	Uses a Digital Tool
1-99 Verses	31%
100-250 Verses	57%
251+ Verses	78%

This makes a solid case for the correlation between the use of tools to help us in our memorization and success in memorization.

The Review Engine here at FAST was a favorite among our community, especially among our most active memorizers—no doubt because it is especially optimized for large numbers of verses. But other tools certainly exist. Tools like Swordscript and RememberMe both happen to have been developed by friends of our ministry and you are welcome to check them out. No doubt other tools exist, as well.

But to encourage you to give our own Review Engine a try, we've put together a list of ten great reasons to check out our tool:

1) It's fast and easy to setup. Just type in your references and go.
2) You can memorize in any translation. If it is not one of our default versions, you can enter any version you want manually. It's a simple cut and paste.
3) The mobile version of our site makes it easy to use any of our tools on any device.
4) The Engine is optimized for heavy memorizers who want to keep up with lots of verses, efficiently.
5) It's fully integrated into all our online Bible classes, and study tools, making the whole experience seamless.
6) We've been optimizing it for years, so it's easier than ever to use while still loaded with features.
7) It automatically tracks and updates your review frequencies for every verse.

8) Everything is cloud based so you never have to worry about changing devices or keeping accounts synced.
9) It gives fun awards and reminders to encourage personal consistency.
10) It's the only tool we can provide any support on! :) And we're definitely here to help!

Actually, I could have made this list a lot longer, by mentioning things like our card generator, our flash card drills, our first letter tools, hundreds of popular verse sets, topical chain referencing, all kinds of custom drills, like reference drills, a reclaim pile, and much more. We've actually got a whole library of tools you can use anywhere, at any time, on any device. And they are all fully integrated across our site.

Oh, and best of all, the Review Engine, like most of our tools, is completely free!

If you have never tried our Review Engine before, we encourage you to give it a look. We've been working hard to make it easy to use and more intuitive than ever—and even have a helpful "Getting Started" welcome tutorial which will walk you right through the setup process. To check it out, just go to the TOOLS on our site (*WWW.FAST.ST*). You'll find links to both the Verse Pack and Review Engine, right there at the top of the page.

It's also super easy way to put a shortcut to these tools right on your phone. Just go to the tool you want to add, then follow the instructions in this tutorial (*http://fast.st/phone*). Create as many shortcuts as you want! One click, and you can get to whatever tool you want in an instant.

Of course, if you are already using another system that works for you, feel free to stick with it.

And if you prefer using a physical verse pack and cards to memorize, that's fine too. We actually have various record keeping forms you can print out designed to help with this. And we even have a snazzy Card Generator you can use to print verse cards in various sizes. The point is, explore around!

Bottom line: you just need a system in place to learn new verses and review old verses consistently. And then to stick with that system! Do these two things regularly, whether on paper or an app, and you'll be off and running in no time!

Two more big keys coming up you won't want to miss. Back again soon...

Engine Magic
Study Questions

Is it possible to memorize successfully without using a digital app of some sort?

Why do you think most good memorizers seem to prefer using a digital app?

What are ten good reasons to give the Review Engine a try?

-
-

-
-

-
-

-
-

-
-

What additional tools can you find at our website to help you if you prefer using cards?

Summarize the bottom line. What are the two things you have to do to memorize successfully:

Additional Notes:

Continuing On
Chapter 6

With what you have learned so far, you have all the tools you need to begin memorizing effectively. You hopefully even have two verses memorized already!

But the real question is not whether you can memorize a few verses, or even whether you can retain them. The real question is whether you will stay consistent in your memorization through the years to come. Two verses a week will become 1000 in ten years—but only if you stick with it. Two verses every week, for ten years. With daily review, well, every day!

It doesn't have to take a lot of time. You can maintain hundreds of verses in just 10 or 20 minutes a day—by gradually advancing verses to weekly, monthly and even quarterly frequencies over time. It's really is doable. In fact, success has nothing to do with intellect, memory, age, or education. It boils down to one thing: consistency.

And the secret to consistency is accountability.

There is something in the nature of man that needs the encouragement and accountability that comes through close fellowship with believers that share your desire to hide the Word in their hearts! You will find the power of accountability critical to lasting success.

Why is it so important? Hebrews tells us to "exhort one another daily . . . lest any of you be hardened through the deceitfulness of sin. For we are made partakers of Christ, if we hold the beginning of our confidence stedfast unto the end" (Hebrews 3:13-14). We may start out with good intentions—but it is all too easy to get discouraged, or distracted.

This idea of exhortation becomes even more important the closer we get to the end. As Hebrews continues a few chapters later: "let us consider one another to provoke unto love and to good works . . . exhorting one another: and so much the more, as ye see the day approaching" (Hebrews 10:24-25). To memorize Scripture as earnestly as we need to in these closing hours of earth's history—we've simply got to get some support!

This is one reason we created our online community at FAST. So you can interact with other memorizers from around the world, take classes, get weekly memos, listen to sermons—whatever helps you the most. We've also got hand-picked verses sets on all sorts of topics, and even a random verse of the day. There's a wealth of resources, and I want to encourage you to plug in.

Even better, gather a few friends in your area—and start meeting with them to set memory goals, and check up on each other. To help you and your friends begin laying up the Word, FAST has developed a number of small group Bible study programs that encourage memorization—as well as other important aspects of the Christian life. We recommend starting with our popular Survival Kit course—which is a five week introduction to memorization. But whether you use one of our courses, or choose something different, gather a few friends together and start memorizing!

If you can't get a group together, see if you can't find someone willing to at least check up on you once a week. Ask God to show you just the right person, then go up to them and say: Hey, I'm really wanting to be consistent with my memorization and I need someone to check up on me and make sure I'm keeping up with new verses every week. Would you be willing to help me? They don't even have to be local, just set a time to get on the phone or connect by video. Then recite your verses. Encourage them to hold you to a high standard, and keep you uplifted in prayer. If they are interested in memorizing too, you can do the same for them.

> Ecclesiastes 4:9-10
> 9 Two are better than one; because they have a good reward for their labour. 10 For if they fall, the one will lift up his fellow: but woe to him that is alone when he falleth; for he hath not another to help him up.

Accountability is the key to consistency. It's just that simple. In fact, it's so important, we've create another tool just for this called the Partners Checklist. I won't say more about it here, but it's in the TOOLS section of our site too, and you are welcome to check it out.

Before closing, here's one more verse we recommend memorizing: Revelation 22:21. It's the last verse of the Bible. I've done seminars on memorization in countless churches and I often ask two questions: Who knows the first verse of the Bible? Lot's of people always do. Then, who knows the last verse of the Bible? I don't think anyone has ever answered that question correctly yet.

That says something about human nature doesn't it? We are good at starting new things, but not so good at finishing them. That's what today's reading is all about. Being faithful to the end. About continuing on. Here's that verse, by the way. Go ahead and memorize it right now:

Revelation 22:21
The grace of our Lord Jesus Christ be with you all. Amen.

It's a great reminder, isn't it? That while commitment is important, good methods are important, accountability is important, and all the rest—ultimately success boils down to the grace of Jesus in our life! Meditate on that while you learn this verse.

Ok, we're almost finished! One more memory secret to go, and we're done...

Continuing On
Study Questions

When it comes to Bible memorization, what is the real question that determines our success or failure?

How many verses will you have in ten years if you just memorize two verses a week?

How many verses can you maintain at just 10 or 20 minutes a day, if you properly advance your verses?

What does the Bible suggest is the key to longterm consistency?

What are some ways you can get encouragement, and support through an online community like FAST?

What are two ways you can get that essential accountability offline?

How important is it to not just be a starter, but also a finisher?

Additional Notes:

Spreading Sparks
Chapter 7

Ready for one last tip? There's a lot more to memorization, of course, than what we've covered so far—but these studies were designed to give you enough of the basics to get you started fast. And today's tip covers the last of those basics. Essentially: it helps to share.

I don't know exactly why this is, but I have had countless people tell me the verses that stick best in their minds are the ones they share with others. Maybe there is something happening in the brain, some neuro transmitter getting triggered. I don't know. But I'm pretty sure there is something to it.

Even those who don't have any kind of systematic memorization program, but simply share their faith regularly, tend to have a good command of Scripture.

Personally, I think God just blesses those who are faithful to share! Notice this verse from the book of Proverbs

> *Proverbs 22:20-21*
> *Have not I written to thee excellent things in counsels and knowledge, that I might make thee know the certainty of the words of truth; that thou mightest answer the words of truth to them that send unto thee?*

Solomon is clearly saying God has given us His Word so we can know truth for our self AND so we can share it with others. When we cooperate with His purposes, He blesses. And by the way, verse 18 says: "It is a pleasant thing if thou keep them [God's Words] within thee; they shall withal be fitted in thy lips." That's memorization! It's fitting God's Word in our lips.

Anyway, look for ways to share every verse you learn. Here's a suggestion:

Go to Facebook or Twitter and say: "I memorized the Bible from beginning to end in just one week. Ask me how..." After all, you have learned at the first and last verse, right? If you want, add something additional like, "Note: I'm still working on some of the verses in the middle..."

Or try saying something like that to a friend, just for fun. Just be sure to put on a big smile when you do! If they say, that's impossible, quote Philippians 4:13. See how useful Scripture memory can be?

Remember I told you I had another reason for having you memorize Genesis 1:1. This is it. It's also why I encouraged you to memorize Revelation 22:21, the last verse of the Bible. Bragging rights. :)

Obviously, you don't want to leave anyone misled or confused. You can quickly explain you took this class at FAST that taught you some basic principles of memorization and you learned both the first and last verse of the Bible in less than one week. And that you have started a journey to learn the rest! Then, point them to our site and encourage them to give this class a try for themself. You never know, it might just "spark" a turning point in their life.

Seriously, sharing is good. Like the old campfire song goes, it only takes a spark...

Unsurprisingly, we have a whole library of resources to help you share our training with others. This time, go to the CLASSES tab, and find the link that says "Sharing Resources". You'll find our Crash Course listed right at the top of that page. We keep that class completely free all year round–so feel free to pass it on!

In summary, the more we allow God's Spirit to work through by, by sharing memorized verses with friends when impressed by the Holy Spirit, the more God seems to seal those verses into our heart. The more we encourage others to start memorizing, the more motivated we will be to keep memorizing ourself.

So get out there and start sharing today. You really do have something worth telling!

And on that note, congrats in advance on finishing up this brief introduction to memorization. It's been great sharing with you!

Spreading Sparks
Study Questions

What is our final key to memorizing Scripture effectively?

Why do you think this seems to make such a difference?

Explain how you can use the verses you've learned in this course to introduce the topic of Bible memorization with a friend?

Where can you go to find sharing resources?

Additional Notes:

The Minute Memorizer
Bonus Resource

Want to get your memorization off to a great start? Work on our list of the 52 best verses you can memorize in under a minute. They are all great verses and just 7 words or less. Learn one a week, or bump it up to one a day, and knock them out faster. Here you go:

2 Words
John 11:35	"Jesus wept."
I Thessalonians 5:16	"Rejoice evermore."

3 Words
Luke 17:32	"Remember Lot's wife."
I Thessalonians 5:17	"Pray without ceasing."
I Thessalonians 5:20	"Despise not prophesyings."

4 Words
Exodus 20:13	"Thou shalt not kill."
Exodus 20:15	"Thou shalt not steal."
I Thessalonians 5:19	"Quench not the Spirit."
I Thessalonians 5:25	"Brethren, pray for us."
Hebrews 13:1	"Let brotherly love continue."

5 Words
Exodus 20:14	"Thou shalt not commit adultery."
Mark 4:14	"The sower soweth the word."
Luke 24:8	"And they remembered his words,"
I Timothy 4:11	"These things command and teach."

6 Words

Matthew 24:25	"Behold, I have told you before."
John 5:41	"I receive not honour from men."
John 6:48	"I am that bread of life."
John 10:30	"I and my Father are one."
John 10:42	"And many believed on him there."
Acts 14:7	"And there they preached the gospel."
Ephesians 4:27	"Neither give place to the devil."
I Thessalonians 5:22	"Abstain from all appearance of evil."
James 1:16	"Do not err, my beloved brethren."

7 Words

Numbers 6:24	"The LORD bless thee, and keep thee:"
Deuteronomy 14:3	"Thou shalt not eat any abominable thing."
Proverbs 27:5	"Open rebuke is better than secret love."
Matthew 3:8	"Bring forth therefore fruits meet for repentance:"
Matthew 6:11	"Give us this day our daily bread."
Matthew 7:1	"Judge not, that ye be not judged."
Matthew 24:8	"All these are the beginning of sorrows."
Mark 14:50	"And they all forsook him, and fled."
Mark 15:13	"And they cried out again, Crucify him."
Luke 1:37	"For with God nothing shall be impossible."
Luke 2:30	"For mine eyes have seen thy salvation,"
Luke 21:19	"In your patience possess ye your souls."
Luke 24:48	"And ye are witnesses of these things."
John 3:30	"He must increase, but I must decrease."
John 14:15	"If ye love me, keep my commandments."
John 16:31	"Jesus answered them, Do ye now believe?"

Acts 13:30	"But God raised him from the dead:"
I Corinthians 10:14	"Wherefore, my dearly beloved, flee from idolatry."
II Corinthians 13:12	"Greet one another with an holy kiss."
Galatians 5:9	"A little leaven leaveneth the whole lump."
Ephesians 5:7	"Be not ye therefore partakers with them."
Philippians 2:14	"Do all things without murmurings and disputings:"
I Thessalonians 1:4	"Knowing, brethren beloved, your election of God."
I Thessalonians 2:20	"For ye are our glory and joy."
I Thessalonians 4:18	"Wherefore comfort one another with these words."
I Timothy 6:6	"But godliness with contentment is great gain."
Hebrews 12:29	"For our God is a consuming fire."
I Peter 4:9	"Use hospitality one to another without grudging."
I John 5:21	"Little children, keep yourselves from idols. Amen."

To share this list with others, point them to this link:

http://fast.st/minmem

FAST Missions
Cutting-Edge Tools and Training

Ready to become a Revival Agent? FAST Missions can help! Our comprehensive training curriculum will give you the skills you need to take in God's Word effectively, live it out practically, and pass it on to others consistently.

Eager to start memorizing God's Word? Our powerful keys will transform your ability to hide Scripture in your heart.

Want to explore the secrets of "real life" discipleship? Our next level training zooms in on critical keys to growth, like Bible study, prayer, time management, and more.

Want to become a worker in the cause of Christ? Our most advanced training is designed to give you the exact ministry skills you need to see revival spread.

For more information, please visit us at:
WWW.FASTMISSIONS.COM

Study Guides

Looking for life-changing study guides to use in your small group or Bible study class? These resources have been used by thousands around the world. You could be next!

Survival Kit
Want to learn how to memorize Scripture effectively? These study guides will teach you 10 keys to memorization, all drawn straight from the Bible. Our most popular course ever!

Basic Training
Discover nuts and bolts keys to the core skills of discipleship: prayer, Bible study, time management, and more. Then learn how to share these skills with others. It is the course that launched our ministry!

Revival Keys
Now as never before, God's people need revival. And these guides can show you how to spark revival in your family, church, and community. A great revival is coming. Are you ready?

Online Classes

Want to try out some of the resources available at FAST? Here is just a small sampling of courses from among dozens of personal and small group study resources:

Crash Course
Discover Bible-based keys to effective memorization.
http://fast.st/cc

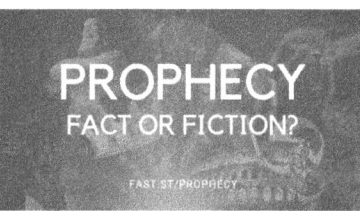

Fact or Fiction
Does the Bible really predict future events? You be the judge.
http://fast.st/prophecy

Monkey Business
Find out how evolution flunks the science test.
http://fast.st/monkey

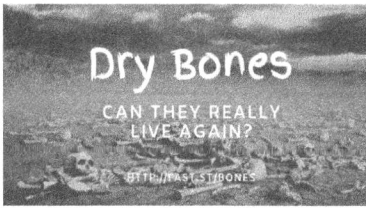

Dry Bones
Want more of God's Spirit? Learn how to pursue revival.
http://fast.st/bones

The Lost Art
Rediscover New Testament keys to making disciples.
http://fast.st/lostart

Digital Tools

FAST offers a number of powerful "apps for the soul" you can use to grow in your walk with God. And many of these are completely free to anyone with an account. Some of these include:

Review Engine
Our powerful review engine is designed to help ensure effective longterm Bible memorization. Give it a try, it works!

Bible Reading
An innovative Bible reading tool to help you read through the entire Bible, at your own pace, and in any order you want.

Prayer Journal
Use this tool to organize important requests, and we'll remind you to pray for them on the schedule you want.

Time Management
Learn how to be more productive, by keeping track of what you need to do and when. Just log in daily and get stuff done.

For more information about more than twenty tools like these, please visit us at *http://fast.st/tools*.

Books

If the content of this little book stirred your heart, look for these titles by the same author.

For Such A Time...
A challenging look at the importance of memorization for the last days, including topics such as the Three Angel's messages and the Latter Rain.

Moral Machinery
Discover how our spiritual, mental, and physical faculties work together using the sanctuary as a blueprint. Astonishing insights that could revolutionize your life!

The Movement
Discover God's plan to finish the work through a powerful endtime movement. Gain critical insights into what lies just ahead for the remnant!